The Paper Wasp

The Paper Wasp

teresa cader

◤■ TRIQUARTERLY BOOKS
■■ NORTHWESTERN UNIVERSITY PRESS

Evanston, Illinois

TriQuarterly Books
Northwestern University Press
www.nupress.northwestern.edu

Printed in the United States of America

10   9   8   7   6   5   4   3   2

ISBN-13: 978-0-8101-5083-6 (cloth)
ISBN-10: 0-8101-5083-2 (cloth)
ISBN-13: 978-0-8101-5084-3 (paper)
ISBN-10: 0-8101-5084-0 (paper)

Library of Congress Cataloging-in-Publication Data

Cader, Teresa.
    The paper wasp / Teresa Cader.
        p. cm.
    ISBN 0-8101-5083-2 (alk. paper). — ISBN 0-8101-5084-0 (pbk. : alk. paper)
    I. Title.
    PS3553.A3134P36 1998
    813.54—dc21
                                                                    98-34132
                                                                    CIP

♾ The paper used in this publication meets the minimum requirements of the
American National Standard for Information Sciences—Permanence of Paper
for Printed Library Materials, ANSI Z39.48-1992.

To my husband, Jerry Mechling,

and my daughters,

Katherine and Emma

contents

Part Two

Part Three

acknowledgments

I am grateful to the editors of the following publications in which the poems listed below first appeared.

Agni: "Spirit Papers," "Three Parables," "A Poetics of Birth," "At the Edge of Being" (sections 6, 9, and 10)

American Literary Review: "An Excuse," "Empty Is My Fullness"

The Atlantic Monthly: "Correspondence," "At the Edge of Being" (section 4, which appeared as "The Odds")

Black Warrior Review: "A Legend of Paper Money"

Descant: "The Sumerian Symbol for Bird," "*Scapula*"

Harvard Magazine: "Can't"

Ploughshares: "Wind, Horse, Snow"

Poetry: "Empress Shōtoku Invents Printing in 770"

Prairie Schooner: "Fists," "A Primer"

Radcliffe Quarterly: "The Task," "At the Edge of Being" (sections 1, 5, 11, and 13)

Slate: "By the River," "*Oeuvre,* Spirulina, Mugwomp"

TriQuarterly: "Six Entries on the Invention of Paper," "Invisible Order," "Atom"

"Internal Exile" won the 1997 George Bogin Memorial Award from the Poetry Society of America.

I would like to thank the National Endowment for the Arts for two fellowships given during the writing of this book. I am especially grateful to the Mary Ingraham Bunting Institute at Radcliffe College for a fellowship year of sustained creativity, intellectual stimulation, and friendship.

The Paper Wasp

THE TASK

I am routing the closet I have neglected for years.
I toss out the broken mirror, the expired
prescriptions, the earring waiting for its lost mate.
I fold linen onto the shelves, remove George Herbert
from the gift bag I'd been hiding under the sheets.
I don't know how to pray. I stare at the empty page
of my soul and wait for something to happen.
I clean closets at midnight to avoid the miraculous,
the engendering of the sacred. Here are pictures
of my daughter at birth, with clear, unblinking eyes:
what is it she can't tell me about being born?
Is there always prayer on the other side of language?
Did she find the seismic shudders terrifying,
the sudden expulsion into light?
You see it, too: the gap that can't be closed.

Part One

SIX ENTRIES ON THE INVENTION OF PAPER

1

It begins with a wasp on a terrace in ancient China:
a man invents paper after watching the wasp
spin its white nest from mulberry bark.

2

Perhaps he has found bamboo too uneven
for letters in black wax.
Perhaps he is weary of verticality.
Perhaps he is ashamed of his private longings.

3

When his neighbor calls to him, "Ts'ai Lun,
what are you boiling in that large pot?"
he does not show him linen rags found in a basket,
old fish nets hauled off the docks,
mulberry bark stripped from the neighbor's tree.

4

His neighbor sees thin sheets of pulp strewn
across the terrace, drying in the sun.

He does not perceive them as treasures.
He is annoyed with the clutter.

His children are forbidden to set foot on the terrace.
He whispers about Ts'ai Lun in the tea shop.

5

One evening after an inquisition at court—
the inventor has been implicated in palace unrest—
Ts'ai Lun comes home, drinks poison, and goes to bed.

6

On a table lie stacks of the white sheets.
The mulberry tree looks seamless in the moonlight.
The wasp is poised to devour some workers at dawn.

SPIRIT PAPERS

While her husband spent his afternoons napping
on the terrace, or vomiting into a spittoon,
Madame Chung visited the paper shops.

A lavender lotus blossom tea set,
two white horses pulling a red chariot,
black robes with gold fire-dragons,

how hard she worked to find them.
Was her husband not worth hours on foot
and the last of her marriage gold?

At the shop of the famous Tien Chi
she ordered an effigy of her husband's dog
and a likeness of herself, smiling.

She ministered to her husband
as spring rains closed the paper shops.
Then his breath became a dried leaf.

"Please serve my husband's tea hot,"
she wrote on the paper tea tray
she placed in front of his coffin.

She lit a torch beneath the dog's jowl.
The dog burst into flame, its head popped.
Smoke circled in black saucers.

Madame Chung watched the white horses
gallop into the sky to meet her husband,
who rose from his chair to greet them.

INVISIBLE ORDER

How ordinary the days were: afternoon rains,
a rash of purple crocuses across the grass,
pear blossoms adrift on the stone fence.

A paper wasp chose the overhang above the patio,
obscured by wisteria and a sycamore.

In grief and weariness we sat on our porch.
She darted between us and the wooden fence
by the grape arbor and we did not thwart her.
We barely recognized her for what she was.

We were inexact about ourselves, too.
How had death taken us so by surprise?

Now we know how hard she labored.
While we rocked in our chairs or dozed,
she sawed and mashed splinters from the fence
and spun a white dome above our heads.

One day we heard a trembling in the eaves
and took our binoculars out:
hundreds of bodies strained against the nest.

In her paper universe she had built an order
slavish to her will, while we, with keen eyes
and ordinary preoccupations, suspected nothing.

She sometimes ate her sluggish offspring,
we later learned, if she got too hungry;
she forbade her daughters to reproduce;
the doomed males fell to their passions.

But on the day we saw that teeming nest up close,
we felt barren in our grief. Lacking words,
we wanted to smash it, to let joy loose on the world.

MASSAGE

The masseuse takes oil from a jar and rubs it on my feet.
She presses her thumb into tangled nerve endings.
Pin-prickles spiral up my calves.

She squeezes the back of my heel, compressing nodules
the size of marbles, palpates fibers along my instep
as knotted as macramé.

If feet are sentinels where the organs of the body
meet, her fingers are tapping out a code
of distress from my heart, anger from my liver.

I think about the body's secrets: what else might
be going on in there without my knowledge?
Why so little trust between us?

Last week my friend received news: two lumps,
small as mustard seeds, impossible to feel.
Where is the kingdom of God in that deception?

And why is the language of the body
so obtuse, an autism of cells incapable of disclosure?
Whom am I addressing? Who is listening?

THREE PARABLES

1. The Paralytic

Pick up your bed, the voice says, and he does,
staggering out of the house, into the book.

Guilt, guilt, guilt the small birds call into the dark
as they wing away from the city.

What is left to forgive, except the bed?

2. Unclean

She touches his hem. Long enough
for the blood to stop, for the power

to leave his body. And where does it go?
She gets up from the ground, exposed,

whole, like a garment drying in the sun.
What happens to the stains?

3. The Bent-over Woman

He sees her, hidden among men
in the Lord's place, on the Sabbath,

and calls her into the light. He lays
his hands on her and she is made straight.

When he breaks the back of the law for her,
what is healed, the law or her back?

THE DEVIL

That you should ask such a question is preposterous.
You inch along the floor like a reptile.
You switch colors when the game is up.
How did I come to know a tongue so venomous,
a backbone that slithers in self-interest?
I do not admire your obsequious pining for insects.
No, I will not. I have too much pride for that.
My first temptation was to enter this conversation.

. . .

You misinterpret my silence.
You imagine that I think the way you do,
always looking for a crack in the wall.
I find that a few words are sufficient.
I thought I made it clear I abhor ambiguity
and I am not swayed by symbols.
That you continue to impose on my reticence
meanings you invent is a form of violence.

. . .

There is no reason to infer such a thing.

The invisible does not belong to you alone.

I can also tempt with skin, with my tongue.

You are most potent among all the creatures.

Even the lion fears your bite.

I will comb the grasses for you.

I will coil myself on the throats of your enemies.

I will swallow every word you utter.

THE SUMERIAN SYMBOL
FOR BIRD

Today I am thinking about cuneiform tablets
stored in clay pots in an ancient Sumerian library
and about a boy aged eight studying to be a scribe
in the temple school, pressing his square-tipped
reed into the clay each morning as he unlearns
his impulse to draw, not write, the bird.

And I am thinking of the middle-aged artist
in the studio across from mine, making peaches
nestle in the folds of a blue and white tablecloth.
On a green wooden table a pewter pitcher
is beaded with drops of water. Nothing disturbs
the peach fuzz whitening in the sun.

The boy memorizes his symbols, and she says
she doesn't read so much these days, she mostly looks.
He must work hard to transform his bird
into the idea of flight. Her peaches are stubborn
in their desire to remain peaches. An open window
allows the white muslin to billow: she closes it.

"The ear of the boy is on his back," an Egyptian
proverb goes. The boy is beaten if he wavers
in the task of disassembling his bird-flight
into a collection of sounds. The artist is distracted
for some reason today. She eats one of the peaches
from a white plate and drinks some cool water.

I stare at the Sumerian symbol for bird, imagining
a wine goblet in its curves, or the metal beams
of a greenhouse. Nothing evokes flight or wings.
Work is over for the day. The boy steps out
of the tablet into the anonymous history of language.
The artist signs her canvas with a boar's-hair brush.

EMPRESS SHŌTOKU INVENTS PRINTING IN 770

Smallpox, insurrection. Was her kingdom not ravaged enough already?
Had the gods of disfigurement not been appeased?

She would not abide, she would not acknowledge impediment.

The priests' advice to order prayer in all the village temples
was enough to excite her mind to invention:

She would construct a million tiny pagodas,
commission architects of the written word

to print dhāranī for each of them
to ward off the demons of disease and war.

Amplified, repeated, the prayers would reach
the ears of Buddha in unison,

so that the loneliness of one priest praying,
the vulnerability of one prayer floating in black ink,

the unpredictability of a scrap of paper against a universe
of rain and wind and wayward candle flame,

might be fashioned into mystical choruses
rising into the air with simultaneous intention.

She would pray for her invention, she would give her priests the vision
to see multiplicity, to make a stone, a block, a metal sheet

empowered to copy whole prayers in rapid succession
like the singing of the stars, the flutter of bamboo leaves.

Were a million dhāranī not a million times more powerful?

And her private prayer, her wish for immortality,
would it not ascend on a million whispering tongues?

A LEGEND OF PAPER MONEY

In the fourteenth century a certain Emperor Wu
tried to save his kingdom from counterfeit money,

which had made even the smallest transactions
among people a matter of great suspicion.

He consulted his advisors, who located the problem
in the paper on which the money was printed.

After meditating for three moons, they announced
a formula for paper impossible to duplicate:

macerate the hearts of the great literary men
of China, then mix with the pulp of mulberry bark.

The Emperor exiled his advisors to the mountains
to breathe jasmine, then sought the Empress,

who was reading under a bamboo trellis.
They paced the bridge above the fishpond,

plotting ways to save the court poet and his friends.
The Empress, known to be very clever, advanced

her own notion that the hearts of great literary men
were to be found in their writings.

The Emperor could not believe his luck.
He dumped all the manuscripts in China into steaming vats

and invited the court poet and his friends to celebrate
the prosperity of the kingdom and their own good fortune.

The ink bled into the pulp, turning it a distinctive gray,
which no counterfeit artist in the kingdom could duplicate.

THE PAPER ARTIST AT WORK

This isn't a painting, this field of dogwoods,
the surface is not a surface, the trees adhere
to the air by mingling fibers with it,

the way white blossoms falling
change the texture of light,
so many filigreed leaves embracing their ribs,

lifting a downy fuzz.
The artist must work quickly:
invisible fibers disintegrate and fuse,

pulp on pulp a profusion of plant tentacles
vining themselves around branch,
or bark, drying into bloom

amid the shattered calm of the sky.

SCAPULA

I listen now for the music,
integument, scapula, interstitial,
not for the argument, the electric

pulse of fact. I let *intercostal*
glide across my teeth,
converse with *musculoskeletal*

and *flexor* on the white table beneath
the laminated diagrams
of bodies perfecting the absence of death.

Dye raced through the milogram's
road map like the 1968 Beetle
we flipped onto its roof. Numb,

my fingertips in leather gloves, brittle
puppets without a puppeteer,
as blood riddled

the cracked windshield. A tear
in the *trapezius,*
cracks in the cervical discs where

movement meets desire. *Subclavius*
leaps from chart to ear,
splenius, gluteus maximus, soleus.

The brace, the reading stand, the traction bar,
an education spent in agony
reading poets my woozy brain couldn't hear.

My head falls into the therapist's hands. My body
feels severed from my mind.
What does this pain, this vulnerability

have to do with the music of *scapula?* Suspended
in weightlessness, I listen to my heart.
Levator, masseter, temporalis pound

in my ears like the first time I heard Mozart,
stealing down the steps at night.

AN EXCUSE

No, today the sap in the maple tree is frozen.
Cords of wood lie unsplit in the shed.
Baskets of white linen mildew in the cellar.

Do not apologize. You did not mean to comply
with disorder; the lamp burning in your study
is testament. Even your body lacks clarity.

There is not much you can do about it.
Guard the key. Hoard the syrup. Sleep little.
Inhabit the clean, unforgiving page.

WIND, HORSE, SNOW

1

The Eskimo children balance their blackboards
on their knees and write with soft fat chalk.

A storm skitters across the frozen sea.
Smidgens of ice have swirled into pinwheels.

2

The painter Magritte is dabbing black paint
on his canvas. Beneath the clock he writes
wind, beneath the door *horse.*

3

The Eskimo children have a new teacher,
from Connecticut, who wants them to learn
a poem about stopping by the woods
on a snowy evening with an intelligent horse.

4

It is summer in the ragweed field.
Magritte says there is no picture without a frame.
When he stares from his attic window, does he see
the field, or a composition of the field?
Is it possible for me to love you
without inventing you?

5

The Eskimo children admire the horse most.

6

The children must pick a word to describe
the snow that batters their windows.
If it is too wet, their fathers might freeze
as they paddle home. If it is dry and powdery,
the dogs can make the run to town for food.

7

"The word dog does not bite,"
observed William James,
who admired Magritte's horse.

8

If my language has no future tense,
am I the same person I was as a child?

Part Two

A POETICS OF BIRTH

I've had trouble finding a way to talk about birth
that would embrace the conditional tense of pregnancy,
the conjunctive logic of conception,
the copulative, antithetical coordinate, death
(which might seem a disjunctive subject),
and birth's metaphorical correlative, art.

Finding the right words is a rarefied art
in a language that can't speak about birth
without making the physical body its only subject,
reduced to the fluids and capillaries of pregnancy,
and severed from the phenomenology of death,
as though birth were not, in etymological origin, conceptual.

With nothing but abortive words to express my conception
of the problem, I'll create a diatribe, not art,
unless I appropriate another lexicon. Death
might do, that shadow partner in birth,
in whom the unknown reveals itself in pregnant
expectation and the invisible becomes the real subject.

But in an art where language itself can be the subject,
why is conceive less powerful than concept,
and "significant, full of meaning," no longer "pregnant"?
If origination and form are the conjunctive conditions of art,
how did artistic power get stripped from birthing?
A polemic, I can hear you say—deadly—

and you're right. Language aside, it's death
to make a poem of ideas, to wantonly subject
the reader (and oneself) to a discourse on birthing.
And believe me, I don't have the slightest conception
of how to get myself out of this mess artfully.
Grammatically speaking, my construction is pregnant.

"My matter hath no voice, but to your own most pregnant
and vouchsafed ear," Shakespeare says of how meaning dies
without an instrument attuned to hearing it. Artistically
speaking, our language here is ectopic, totally subjective,
incapable of conjoining the literal and conceptual.
In Auden's tome of famous quotes, there are none on birth.

The imagination (once a definition of pregnant) is my subject,
and its muse, death, although when I began I didn't conceive
it that way. I tried to write about art and birth.

C A N ' T

Can't. A contraction.
The curtain hangs in a circle around her.
She fixes her attention on one spot:
The mind is a white field, cleared of pain.

Hanging in a circle around her, the curtain
divides her from the world she knows.
She wants to be *a white field, cleared of pain.*
She wants to remember her instructor's words.

Dividing her from the world she knows,
pain has left her speechless, stunned.
She wants to remember her instructor's words
about becoming pain's instrument, its accomplice.

Leaving her speechless and stunned, pain
enters the white field, demands to possess it.
Not to become its instrument, its accomplice,
she concentrates on her breath.

Enter the white field, demand to possess it,
she remembers as she watches the monitor.
She concentrates on her breath.
She observes her pain, then releases it.

She remembers, as she watches the monitor,
how to fix her attention on one spot.
Observing her pain, she releases its
can't, her body's contraction.

BY THE RIVER

He watched her thrash in the reeds like a horned four-leg.
Her body cracked and trembled like the ground opening.
She breathed on the surface of it. She slipped beneath it.
Then it pulled her under. She was the river
and he was on the bank of the river as it rose around him.

There was an opening. A gateway. She disappeared
behind it. The center split wide. He heard the earth groan.
The shores of her body overflowed and she drowned in herself.
His breath whistled in his chest. He was sucked into her.
She would spit him up into the reeds.

The sky was wailing. The river was receding.
Through her lips the earth called and he could not answer.
Then it broke, the waters calmed, he heard the cry and saw the one
who had come from her. The body was like his, not hers,
and yet was not of him. He knelt beside them, alone.

FISTS

All night wind rattled, branches scraped the eaves.
I am not a magician. I did not know who knocked.

I slept in gusts, breathed cups of air.
The caller would not be turned away. The night hung

in the sky, a giant weight suspended above the earth.
Do not ask me what I knew about myself.

I stared at the lilacs, saw the tiny globes explode.
Perhaps I was crying, or my breath was sucked inward.

I could not rise from the bed, stop the fists.
Then the door collapsed, wind whirled through the room.

In that whoosh I vanished. On the bed lay the body
I had inhabited. I looked with awe, but I was weightless now,

almost an idea floating above my body: *mother,*
holding an other, and I knew nothing of where I was.

AT THE EDGE OF BEING

I

Under the microscope they pursue me:
seven tail-wagging spermatozoa.
I feel eighteen again and sensual,
pulling my skirt above my sunburned knee,
twisting my bare shoulders casually.
He's the boy on the cottage veranda,
sipping vodka with lime and papaya.
The breeze burns with possibility.
The doctor sears the slide with a single match.
A variegated fern blossoms there
in the opulent milk of mucus and sperm.
I pull my husband close so we can watch
the veins drying to life in that estral air,
our harvest cupped in someone else's palms.

2

Without inflection, we say, meaning without
emotion, and the specialist's voice is flat:
the egg drops here, the sperm swim up,
the whole thing happens just like that.
(We're ten years old again, we find the facts
of life in plastic dummies the school nurse hides.)
The luteal phase, a radioactive map
of errant cells, the sluggish tails, all beside
the point: he owns the words for failure,
owns the proof. His words decline
without informing us of misbehavior.
We'd hoped, he says, medically inclined
to skip the present tense and conjugate
us into a past he (consciously?) creates.

3

Distrust the body, my mother tells me,
distrust the weather of blood, menstrual
or accidental, distrust the alchemy
of cells, heretics within the orders
of tissue and bone. Distrust the swelling
and the shrinkage, the cleaving and the loss.
Distrust the neurons because they cannot lie,
the synapses where messages are lost.
Distrust the fruit and the womb, the apple
and the eye that sees it, for vision
is always revision. Distrust the supple
and the stiff, the birthmark and the lesion,
the doors of the temple when they open,
letting the mortal world in.

✝

We watch TV from bed, on satin sheets.
The hockey game is a dead heat;
our team will not relinquish hope despite
the dismal odds. By midnight
the score gets worse, cramped muscles fail,
the lines get slack, the coaches rail
against the referees, and time is running out.
But champions are made without
the normal fear of loss, and ours slog
on with bloodied shins and pockets clogged
with ice. Desperate, we run the clock ourselves:
we scallop, fillip, sweep then delve,
we burrow, borrow, bellow, bless,
rend, render, root without rest.

ʃ

On a cold Saturday morning, I twirl
a vial beside my bedroom window at dawn.
In clear liquid a blue beacon unfurls.
Across the snow-smattered lawn
a chipmunk scurries. The first car sputters out
of a driveway. A neighbor's shower
screeches on. The syntactical arrives by arrangement,
or random luck. But what possibility do I harbor,
its grip tenuous and subordinate?
What am I creating even as the sun
slips across the window ledge, late
in the morning, spilling ficus shadows on the green
rug? I study the test stick's blue ray,
but it has said all that it can say.

6

When the doctor rubs hot jelly below
my navel and slides the metal cone
across my skin, the gray monitor glows
like a granular plateau on the moon.
I hold my breath as sound waves sink
deeper. We graze unyielding ground
until we uncover the heart, a light blinking
where we had seen only darkness. Sound-
less, spectral, shimmering, less
bloodlike than a bloodroot. A signal
is emitted from a lighthouse, but who is lost?
What sea is navigated in that cylindrical
stalk? If I am not the shore,
how can I call anything to come here?

7

My invisible claimant,
you already know the way of flesh,
cells dividing, multiplying, remnant
of reptilian consciousness.
If the wing doesn't sprout,
if the spinal cord doesn't close
In the dark I imagine routes
of escape, closets
through which I disappear into fields
where unicorns stomp their hooves.
As you scale the chromosomal watershed,
I lose my appetite, my love
of particulars. Animal limbs protrude
in dreams, lungs implode.

8

But you, late-term, resemble
a child on the screen, your fingers
and toes intact, your sex dissembled.
The ultrasound's touch is nimble,
the light we saw before is now a chambered
heart, iambic in its intent.
Visible finally, your body is numbered
on a graph, your pertinent
stats recorded. We turn up the sound—
a beat so fast I get dizzy listening,
a jazz drum swishing in the background.
Am I audience or artist, accompanying
you on this stage?
Or do I supply the page?

9

They say grammar is innate, the mind stores
nouns and verbs in separate drawers
like socks and underwear.
If it's true the instinct for language is wired
into our brains, I must harbor
speech in my silence, ardor
in my apathy.
This fractured narrative engulfs me.
How peculiar to be the main character
and its author,
indispensable,
my voice singular but multiple,
creator and created,
out of myself, remade.

10

Because the body is form to its own forgetting,
I spend the summer pacing in the garden,
mute and mindless, my stomach hardened
into silence. Like a yogi, I practice letting
go, but images of white clouds
do not comfort me. Animal will
has taken over. I am all physical,
I am beyond the reach of words.
Is this how the spirit fails?
To be flesh,
to be making flesh of my own flesh—
I am pulled
back into the earth's roster, a skeleton
washing to shore in a pool of plankton.

II

Fear. Its syntax. Subordinate clauses,
as in, *When the contractions begin,*
or, *Six a.m., as winter light pauses*
on the duvet. The way bloodied water runs
in rivulets down the sheets. I turn
the bed lamp on, twist to see the time.
I feel my back flatten out, then curve
as your head burrows downward, in line
with the stretched aperture through which you
will surface, mottled and breathless.
The qualifying pain misconstrued
as symmetry, as in how long its absence lasts.
Eternity in that explosion, not
time. Beginning of the known.

12

In the hospital, on the fourteenth floor,
I listen to the operating room doors
swing open, snap shut.
In a tiny room like the pocket
of an Advent calendar, I float
between body and breath, flat
on my back. Animal, flesh,
perishable. They wash
my face with cloths, the needle soars
across the paper. One peak. No, more—
They put ice chips on my parched tongue.
What can I hold onto?
Is this what it is to die, to be
forced out of the body?

13

I hover above my body, observe
myself laboring. I repeat
with concentration: *observe*
so that you can remember, repeat
so that you can describe.
I am the gate opening, the passageway,
the instrument, the vehicle, alive
to myself at the edge of being. I am day
and night, river and shore,
dying and being born,
witness to the body and soul, the here
and not here, the visible and invisible, the in-
carnate life, known and unknowable, the mystery beyond
mind, beyond body, place where the universe begins.

ᛁᚦ

Suddenly the pain stops,

the pressure gives way.

I hear your startled cry

as the doctor lifts you up,

shaking, bloodied, slippery.

He suctions meconium from your nose.

Nurses towel off a whitish ooze.

With a quick slice you're free.

Your bright blue eyes scan

my face, almost quizzical,

as if *I* were the miracle.

I want to know what you can't

tell me about being born,

what you can never experience again.

A PRIMER

That night I saw Death hovering on a branch outside my window.

Later, he said. *I have not come for you. And have not come for the child.*

But why was he here amid the songs and flowers, the gifts of silver and satin?

Why was he here when pain called to him from a room on the fifth floor,

when families waited for him in the chapel with Bibles on their laps,

when the ambulance screeching uptown was coming just for him?

I looked into the face of my daughter, her blue eyes wide, unblinking.

She had come to me from amniotic sleep, from the dark; she would never

remember that expulsion into light, the way lamps above the receiving table

hurt her eyes and wet towels made her shiver in the cool air.

Death looked in at us both: *I gave birth to her. And to you. When the moon*

is invisible, it is not absent. What you see in the night sky is the day beginning.

Then the branch trembled and he was gone. I heard the ambulance door open.

EMPTY IS MY FULLNESS

I

An antique maple cradle, carried here
in the hull of a British ship, awaits
my daughter's sleep. She stirs
with each motion of my foot.
The creaking wood, limed with linseed oil,
moans its lullaby without apology.
How many infants buried on this soil
survived months at sea
in salt-soaked cabins, or in steerage,
then lay by winter fires with rattled
breath, feverish eyes? Ravaged,
those mothers rocked their cradles
until seams were wrung from maple
staves and the sheets ceased to rustle.

II

Waking to your cry from a fitful sleep,
I turn you over in your bassinet
and listen to you cough so deeply
the blankets shudder. Sweat
glistens on your bare scalp, your fontanel
pulses beneath a skim coat of water
and skin. I peel
off your sleeper, tuck the thermometer
into your ear, your head pressed into me.
I kneel in the light cast by a streetlamp
and cradle you, sobbing, on my knee.
I have no breath, no spell to help
you breathe. I hold you up to the light
and ask it to be what I am not.

III

Your cradle stands empty in my office,
empty the air, the molecules of heat
from the radiator turned up last night.
Empty the floor's creaking surfaces,
the hall of cries muffled by latticed
blankets, even the sunlight
polishing maple staves to a bright
syrupy hue, the desk with its lists
of things not done. Without you, empty
is my fullness, my measure, the cup
I run over and disappear from.
If you were gone, what would I be?
A face at the gate, an empty lap,
a homing bird with no home.

CORRESPONDENCE

"I hat you," my daughter writes
in her newfound mastery of phonics.
She has taken to sending me notes
from kindergarten: love notes,
joke notes, problem notes,
and now angry notes that say
I don't care about her feelings.
These notes arrive after lunch
in envelopes, like the mail,
marked by hearts or skulls.
You are "meen," she says today,
you just sit around and "rit"
and don't let me watch "moves."
Why do her notes carry more weight
than her spoken accusations?
She isn't the same child now:
she is an owner, a thief.

OEUVRE, SPIRULINA, MUGWOMP

I

Play dates, player piano, playbill, Shakespeare's plays,
my younger daughter can't say play, only pay. So she pays
and pays with fervent concentration, while I work and work

and worry the day away. One does not work the piano,
or the violin. One does not create a body
of play. An *oeuvre* we call it, not her life's play, not the drive

that kindled, or destroyed, or turned to gold the impulse,
threaded to the bone like a nerve path, that wild desire to let
the work play itself out, regardless of the price.

II

Spirulina, food of the sea, urchin-fodder, source,
photosynthetic blossom-leaf, dredged
from the deep cold waters where humpbacks

gully and sing, you surface beside the toothpaste
like an accusation at a funeral. Swallow you
and I will learn the secrets floating in those depths,

cell-derived, inscrutable intelligence, eons old,
evolving in fluid concupiscence, flesh of my flesh.

III

Mugwomp, my older daughter announces from the back seat.
Or does she mean mugwump? Bolter from the Republican
Party in 1884, independent in politics, or captain?

Mugwomp, she says clearly, I love the sound of mugwomp.
Swamp, hump, humpback, tug, slug, the pilfered sounds
roll in the wake of her tongue, slashed from their moorings.

Part Three

INTERNAL EXILE

from the journals of Eugenia Ginzburg,
Russian historian and poet

Just remembering it all to record it later had been the main object
of my life throughout those eighteen years. . . . When I began work on
the book, the only landmarks in the labyrinth of the past were my own
poems, also composed without the benefit of pencil or paper.

—*Within the Whirlwind*

1. How It Happened

You are ironing in the dining room,
Paul is reading to Alyosha at the table,
Vasya sleeps in the nursery.
Is this how it happened?—
The phone rings and everyone freezes.
Paul knows, Alyosha knows.
You answer, Yes, yes, of course,
I'll come in at once.
You gather your things quickly.
Alyosha goes out to ice skate,
does not say good-bye.

Vasya screams, Mommy, don't go.
You turn away from him,
slam the door hard.
You walk partway with Paul,
who tells you not to worry,
you'll be home soon.
Then he screams, Genia!
You walk out of your life
on an ordinary, sunny day.
Today, for instance.
Everything you love, gone.
The faces you will not see again.
And you know it.
And you walk on.

2. The Summons

The year 1937 began at the end of 1934:
it was the first of December, four a.m.,
Alyosha and Vasya sleeping with their heads
beneath blankets, light snow falling on Kazan.
Summoned to party headquarters by six,
you slipped your wool dress over your head.
Knotting a flowered shawl beneath your collar,
you stooped to kiss the blankets,
to listen for Alyosha's congested breathing.
Black syrup, hot tea, compresses. . . .
You clicked the door behind you,
opened the gate, breathing the snowlit morning.
The scrape of a shovel, the stomp of boots,
a razor's edge of white light on the horizon,
behind thick velvet curtains a lamp glowing
in a parlor, ice crinkling on your gloves,
the rustlings of a city awakening.
Kirov had been shot by a Communist!
Were they mad? The room was hushed.
Comrades with frozen lips, frightened eyes.
A moment in history, turning, toward what?

3. Momentum

Night after night, cars pulling up to the house,
a man on the corner watching, your drapes
pulled open as if to say, See, here I am,
a simple woman with my children,
here in the darkest part of winter I make a fire,
I draw a bath for my sons, I scrub the dishes
and sip tea. Look at my bookshelves,
my life is written there. My history
is your history. There is no past worth saving,
the road to my house winds through fields
where my people slaved, your people died.
I hide nothing, not even my belief in you.
This will pass. Professor Elvov warned me
to be careful because I didn't denounce his book.
You have taken my job, my party membership,
but I am here before you, as transparent
as the voile framing the window. Am I not
as Russian as you? Am I not your comrade?

4. Lyadsky Park

Sometimes Paul was gone for hours, the scrape
of his boots on the porch beneath your window
waking you at two or three. Then his cold back,
his refusal to answer your questions about the meetings
where you were denounced, Enemy of the People,
Trotskyite, meetings where your friends pored
through your writings to find a word, a phrase,
a slip of logic, an opening. One night you took him
for a walk in Lyadsky Park while the children slept
and the moon polished sleigh tracks in the streets.
You cursed Yaroslavsky. You pleaded, wept.
You raised your hand, as if to strike. Soundlessly
the gold watch snapped off your wrist, dropped
into a snowdrift. You saw a glittering planet
in the night sky, a star hurtling toward earth,
a sliver of light in a field of iridescence.
Together you bent to dig, but the gold watch
had disappeared, its hands frozen in the snow.

S. Pushkin

Three floors underground in a windowless cell,
their words echo like the scuttle of rats.
Sign here. Recant now. Your sons are waiting.
Waiting by the stove, at the door.
Through the dank corridors, footsteps, keys
turning a lock. Howls. A door slams.
Who could you call, what name belonged
to that darkness? What power could keep
the rats from crawling up your arm as you slept?
Mind turning on itself, spiraling to the center,
which must stop spinning—
air dissolving into waves of fractured light—
On the floor, tied up with white towels,
your head bruised from beating, your face swollen,
you had a vision of the poet at his desk, quill in hand,
offering you the silver feet of ballerinas,
bakers in dusty white caps,
a slender neck with feathered ringlets.
You tapped out a message to him in your head:
"All my losses are here beside me, except you,
whom I alone can keep alive."

6. Elgen Forest

On frostbitten feet, in wet boots,
trying to aim the ax,
a sprinkle of chips on the ground,
and the commandant screaming;
missing your quota and losing
an equal percentage of your rations,
weaker each day from not eating,
sleeping in an unheated shack
on wet logs, without buckets or light;
slipping farther from your quota,
forced deeper each day into the forest
in blizzard conditions, in ice,
hands too numb to lift the ax;
and then a thawed patch of snow
in May, a sprig of five or six berries
so red they looked black,
crushing them against your palate,
bittersweet, delicious.

7. Intellectuals

You stood in the center of the chicken house,
balancing a pail of feed above your head,
remembering the saying,
"Even a chicken will bully the sad and the shy."
They swooped from their perches,
cowling and cackling, they pecked
at your bare calves, clawed at your head.
They lit on your shoulders, nipped your ears.
Andronova, the senior poultry keeper,
hated intellectuals, hated anyone
who couldn't keep her chickens alive.
As you bent over the troughs,
they knocked the pail from your hands.
Then you heard it—the thud
of bodies falling from their perches,
the thud that could send you back to the forest,
or worse. You took the hatchet,
whacked the heads from three chickens
already freezing on the sawdust floor
and held them by the tails until the blood
came trickling out of the carcasses.
"Harder! Harder! The more they bleed
the better!"—it was Andronova with a pot.

That's when you learned how to handle
chickens in captivity: Get them
when they look thoughtful,
about to plummet from their perches,
and chop off their heads.

8. Siege of Leningrad

All night the women whispered in their bunks,
news from the war you were not allowed to fight.
The fires in Leningrad, smoke billowing behind barriers
no army could penetrate. And the starved, the dying.
Children dying. To fear your child is starving,
to sense before you are told, that he is dead.
Alyosha, who wouldn't say good-bye, whose skates
glinted in the sunlight as he circled the pond,
pretending not to see you leave.
His fur boots and sheepskin coat, his black eyes.
When did it happen, last week or three weeks ago?
Were you sleeping, were you chopping wood,
were you mashing a raw egg into your rice?
Did anyone stop to help, to mourn?

9. Blizzard

Grief swirling, descending weight,
treetops obliterated, tracks without trace.
Swallowed up, buried continuously, the road
to Izvestkovaya was your pilgrimage.
One false step, one moment of indecision,
and the guard would shoot without warning.
Kilometers measuring your temptation:
the deep, sweet bed of snow, wind-swept
like the white comforter you plumped up
each morning as goose feathers floated
to the cold floor in shafts of sunlight,
comforter for a sleep without nightmares.
One foot before the other, is this the way
Russia would march to its death, the plodding
pace of the defeated? The footsteps
of Akhmatova, Tsvetaeva, Mandlestam?
Who could march them into silence,
keep the music of their boot soles
from reaching the windy steppes,
the curtained parlors of Moscow?
And who could silence them in your mind?
Not all the guards in all the camps,
and not *this* one, with his gun cocked.

10. Anton

Hundreds of species of meadowsweet
with perfect white panticles, pink corymbs,
a field of fireweed with succulent honey.
Knee-deep in blossoms, you shouted the names
in Russian, German, Latin, bending to bless
your rawhide baskets, the herbs snipped clean
at the stems. You had forgotten summer,
its white shroud of sun, the luminescent grasses
cooled by the runoff from the spring snows.
When Anton lifted you into the air and whispered
above the indifferent ears of the taiga,
"Amor mea, mea vita, mea spes,"
you saw the stems of the purple loosestrife
lengthen into fine goblets, until you stood
in a field drunk with sparkling wine and tipped
your heads to its wild and brief stupor.

II. Bach

Maybe you were washing laundry, rolling dough,
an exile in Siberia, a woman with her drapes drawn,
listening for steps on the landing. Maybe you had woken
the night before, crying for Alyosha, and Anton had stroked
your hair, wiped your tears. And now you were sluggish,
unprepared for Vasya as he snapped the shutters open.
Vasya, who came back to you as a young man,
who recited poems that first night as if they were a secret code.
How did you keep yourself from the second loss, turning life
into death, making of Vasya a mausoleum in which to bury Alyosha?
And then the radio blaring: Comrade Iosif Vissarionovich Stalin
is dead of a stroke. The dough in your hands, the wet shirts,
the pages of your journal tucked under your mattress, the face
of Alyosha reassembled in that light-dissembling fugue.

12. Gladioli, 1954

At the Lily of the Valley Café in Moscow,
you sipped black tea, broke your piroshki
into pieces, Siberian piroshki you had loved
twenty years ago when it was fashionable
to choose exotic foods from the east,
when you sat for hours arguing with friends,
critiquing each other's papers and books.
Now the café was jammed with gray-haired
exiles like you, summoned to 41 Kirov Street,
to the General Prosecutor's Office at 2:00.
The café buzzed like a transit camp.
Hands gnarled at Elgen, teeth loosened by scurvy.
Furtive eyes, blank eyes, eyes milky
with cataracts. Where would this journey
end, what more could be taken away?
You noticed the young couple next to you,
staring, their faces shining with tears.
You looked away, ashamed. The woman rushed
for the door, then reappeared at your table
with gladioli wrapped in cellophane.
The café was hushed. Plates rattled in the kitchen.
"We're not heroes, we're victims," someone shouted.
Days later a piece of paper set you free.

"If you lose it, it will not be replaced,"
the colonel warned, then reinstated you in the party.
"In the absence of any corpus delicti," it read.
In the absence of logic, in the absence
your life had become. Two decades gone.
When you wrote about all of this,
did you think your words could change anything?

ATOM

We leave here barefoot, carrying maps we cannot use.

Come to the valley where stars illuminate the night:
our atoms are forged in that fire. We see ourselves transformed.

The day is here when we see galaxies with our naked eye.
That long descent into the body is our first death. Why fear
any other? Numinous accidents comprise our lives.

Let the gods embellish their stories with grails and bones.
We can indulge them anything we choose.

The universe is our fingernail, our obsessive thought.

notes

The poems in *The Paper Wasp* that concern the invention of paper, writing, and printing were written with the help of historical information found in many sources, but particularly in *Papermaking: The History and Technique of an Ancient Craft* by Dard Hunter and *The Origins of Writing,* edited by Wayne M. Senner.

"Internal Exile"

Eugenia Ginzburg, Russian history professor and poet, was sentenced to prison in 1937 for the "crime" of not denouncing a colleague's writings. A loyal Communist, she did not anticipate the extensive brutality and paranoia that would characterize Stalin's reign after the assassination of Kirov. She spent eighteen years in various prisons, camps, and rehabilitation centers in Siberia, many of them in hard labor. She destroyed manuscripts of her own poetry in self-protection. She was reinstated in the Communist Party in 1955 (although not at her request) and later published her journals, *Journey into the Whirlwind* and *Within the Whirlwind,* to international acclaim. Ginzburg's husband, Pavel Vasilyevich Aksyonov, is referred to in the poem as Paul, as he is in her translated journals. The man she later loved, a German Catholic doctor named Anton Walter, was imprisoned with her in Siberia. Her older son, Alyosha, was sent to a home for the children of political prisoners and died. Her surviving son, Vasya, became a writer.